HOW TO USE YOUR BIBLE

Reproducible Activities

GRADES
3–8

CONCORDIA PUBLISHING HOUSE · SAINT LOUIS

Copyright © 2014 Concordia Publishing House
3558 S. Jefferson Avenue
St. Louis, MO 63118-3968

Prepared by Kaellyn Marrs and Rodney L. Rathmann

This publication may be available in Braille, in large print, or on cassette tape for the visually impaired. Please allow 8 to 12 weeks for delivery. Write to Lutheran Braille Workers, P.O. Box 5000, Yucaipa, CA 92399; call toll-free 1-800-925-6092; or visit the website: www .LBWinc.org.

Manufactured in the United States of America

1 2 3 4 5 6 7 8 9 10   23 22 21 20 19 18 17 16 15 14

About This Book

The Bible is a holy book. We call it holy because it contains a message from the holy, all-powerful, and all-knowing God to us. It tells us about God and His love. It tells us about Jesus, the Son of God and Savior of the world. The Bible even tells us about itself.

This resource for teachers contains a variety of reproducible activities that may be used to train students to read and understand the Bible better. These activities guide students in explaining the four different kinds of literature that constitute the Holy Bible. Plus, they familiarize students with study resources such as Bible dictionaries, concordances, cross-references, study notes, and more while providing practice in using them.

The tools and skills they will learn will aid students in their use of the Bible for the rest of their lives. We hope this resource will bless both you and your students as you continue to grow in and through God's holy Word.

God's Word—The Bible

Written by the hands of over forty people over a period of thousands of years, the Bible is really a collections of sixty-six individual books put together in one volume, divided into two parts—the Old and New Testaments.

Many Old Testament books were written by prophets who warned about sin and its consequences while pointing people through messianic promise to the Savior who would one day be born. Some New Testament books tell of the birth, life, death, and resurrection of Jesus, the promised Savior. Others include letters called *epistles*, which answer questions about what it means to live for God. Still, the Bible is really God's Word because God the Holy Spirit gave human writers the very words, thoughts, and ideas to record.

Both Old and New Testaments are filled with wisdom, but God's wisdom is often different from the wisdom of the world. Through this same Word, God's Spirit brings people to faith. He works through His Law to bring people to a know of their sin and through the Gospel to forgive and save them with the Good News of Jesus and His love.

Directions: **Review information provided above about the Bible.** Fill in the blanks to complete the sentences below. Use the words from the word list. You will use one word more than once.

Word List:		
Law	wisdom	Bible
prophets	messianic	epistles
faith	Gospel	Holy Spirit

1. The central message of the _____ is God's plan of salvation through faith in Christ Jesus.

2. Those Bible passages that show us our sin and point out our need for forgiveness are referred to as the _____.

3. Those Bible passages that tell the Good News that we are saved by God's grace through faith in Jesus Christ are referred to as the _____.

4. Old Testament promises of the coming Savior are called _____ promises.

5. The Holy Spirit works saving _____ through the power of God's Word.

6. The messengers who share God's Word may be very different from one another, but each has the same helper, God's _____.

7. God's Word also provides _____ to help us make good decisions about the way that we live our lives. The Bible's _____ (same word as before) is often different from what the world teaches.

8. God used _____ to warn the people about their future if they refused to repent, and to foretell the coming of the Savior.

9. The _____ were letters written to individuals or congregations to answer questions and to strengthen their faith.

Introduction to the Books of the Bible

The Bible tells us about Jesus. The writers of the Old Testament books looked forward to the Savior's promised coming. The writers of the New Testament look back on Jesus Christ's life, death, and resurrection and what His coming means to those who love Him. Study the chart below and answer the following questions.

1. Who wrote the first five books of the Bible? _____

2. Name the five historical books of the New Testament _____ , _____, _____ , _____ , and _____

3. Who wrote most of the epistles found in the New Testament? _____

4. Name two Old Testament books named for the women whose stories they contain. _____ and _____

5. What type of book is the Book of Job? _____

The 39 Books of the Old Testament

The Pentateuch—the five books written by Moses
Genesis
Exodus
Leviticus
Numbers
Deuteronomy

Poetic Books
Job
Psalms
Proverbs
Ecclesiastes
Song of Solomon

Historical Books
Joshua
Judges
Ruth
1 Samuel
2 Samuel
1 Kings
2 Kings
1 Chronicles
2 Chronicles
Ezra
Nehemiah
Esther

Prophetic Books
Major Prophets
Isaiah
Jeremiah
Lamentations
Ezekiel
Daniel

Minor Prophets
Hosea
Joel
Amos
Obadiah
Jonah
Micah
Nahum
Habakkuk
Zephaniah
Haggai
Zechariah
Malachi

The 27 Books of the New Testament

Historical Books
Matthew
Mark
Luke
John
Acts

Epistles by Paul
Romans
1 Corinthians
2 Corinthians
Galatians
Ephesians
Philippians
Colossians
1 Thessalonians
2 Thessalonians
1 Timothy
2 Timothy
Titus
Philemon

General Epistles
Hebrews
James
1 Peter
2 Peter
1 John
2 John
3 John
Jude

Prophetic Books
Revelation

Abbreviations for Books of the Bible

Review the abbreviations that follow.

Book	Abbr.	Book	Abbr.
Genesis	Ge	Habakkuk	Hab
Exodus	Ex	Zephaniah	Zep
Leviticus	Lev	Haggai	Hag
Numbers	Nu	Zechariah	Zec
Deuteronomy	Dt	Malachi	Mal
Joshua	Jos	Matthew	Mt
Judges	Jdg	Mark	Mk
Ruth	Ru	Luke	Lk
1 Samuel	1Sa	John	Jn
2 Samuel	2Sa	Acts	Ac
1 Kings	1Ki	Romans	Ro
2 Kings	2Ki	1 Corinthians	1Co
1 Chronicles	1Ch	2 Corinthians	2Co
2 Chronicles	2Ch	Galatians	Gal
Ezra	Ezr	Ephesians	Eph
Nehemiah	Ne	Philippians	Php
Esther	Est	Colossians	Col
Job	Job	1 Thessalonians	1Th
Psalms	Ps	2 Thessalonians	2Th
Proverbs	Pr	1 Timothy	1Ti
Ecclesiastes	Ecc	2 Timothy	2Ti
Song of Solomon	SS	Titus	Ti
Isaiah	Isa	Philemon	Phm
Jeremiah	Jer	Hebrews	Heb
Lamentations	La	James	Jas
Ezekiel	Eze	1 Peter	1Pe
Daniel	Da	2 Peter	2Pe
Hosea	Hos	1 John	1Jn
Joel	Joel	2 John	2Jn
Amos	Am	3 John	3Jn
Obadiah	Ob	Jude	Jude
Jonah	Jnh	Revelation	Rev
Micah	Mic		
Nahum	Na		

Now fold the paper in half so that only this side of the paper is showing. Write the book of the Bible identified by each of the following abbreviations.

1. Ac _____

2. Am _____

3. Da _____

4. Dt _____

5. Ecc _____

6. Eze _____

7. Ezr _____

8. Ge _____

9. Hos _____

10. Jn _____

11. La _____

12. Ob _____

13. Na _____

14. Ne _____

15. Nu _____

16. Php _____

17. Phm _____

18. Pr _____

19. Ps _____

20. SS _____

It's All about Style

Prompted and directed by the Holy Spirit, writers of the Old Testament originally wrote their words in Hebrew and Aramaic. New Testament writers wrote in Greek. But all wrote by verbal inspiration, a process by which God the Holy Spirit gave them the very thoughts and words they recorded.

Still, the books of the Bible differ in style even as they differ in human writer, purpose, and content.

In all, the books of the Bible can be categorized into the following four distinct styles.

Prophecy—presenting what is happening or will happen in the future.
Apocalyptic—using symbols and codes to convey a message.
Poetry—providing information using rhyme or repetition
Narrative—relating story events in a factual way.

As we read any of these styles of writing found in God's Word, the Holy Spirit helps us rightly to understand and apply them in our life. Consider each of the following Bible verses. In the blank before each of these, write the style (Prophecy, Apocalyptic, Narrative, or Poetry) it most closely represents.

_____ Exodus 13:17–18: "When Pharaoh let the people go, God did not lead them by way of the land of the Philistines, although that was near. For God said, 'Lest the people change their minds when they see war and return to Egypt.' But God led the people around by the way of the wilderness toward the Red Sea. And the people of Israel went up out of the land of Egypt equipped for battle."

_____ Psalm 136:1–2: "Give thanks to the Lord, for He is good,
for His steadfast love endures forever.
Give thanks to the God of gods,
for His steadfast love endures forever
Give thanks to the Lord of lords,
for His steadfast love endures forever."

_____ Ezekiel 26:3–5: "Therefore thus says the Lord God: Behold, I am against you, O Tyre, and will bring up many nations against you, as the sea brings up its waves. They shall destroy the walls of Tyre and break down her towers, and I will scrape her soil from her and make her a bare rock. She shall be in the midst of the sea a place for the spreading of nets, for I have spoken, declares the Lord God. And she shall become plunder for the nations."

_____ Revelation 1:12–16: "Then I turned to see the voice that was speaking to me, and on turning I saw seven golden lampstands, and in the midst of the lampstands one like a Son of man, clothed with a long robe and with a golden sash around His chest. The hairs of His head were white, like white wool, like snow. His eyes were like a flame of fire, His feet were like burnished bronze, refined in a furnace, and His voice was like the roar of many waters. In His right hand he held seven stars, from His mouth came a sharp two-edged sword, and His face was like the sun shining in full strength."

Law and Gospel

Messages of Law and Gospel

God's Word contains two great doctrines, Law and Gospel. The Law tells us what God wants us to do and how He wants us to live. Because we are sinners, it shows us our need for a Savior. The Gospel, on the other hand, tells us what God has done for us in Christ Jesus to forgive and save us.

Read each of the following Bible references. Determine whether the words tell about how God would have people live and act and His punishment of sin (Law), or whether they tell about His love and deliverance—the help and forgiveness He provides to us and to all people through Christ Jesus, His Son, our Savior (Gospel). Write each reference in a appropriate sign on the bottom right of this page.

* Daniel 12:1–3
* Isaiah 42:20
* Jeremiah 23:5–6.
* Amos 9:9–10
* 1 John 1:7
* Ecclesiastes 7:20
* John 3:16

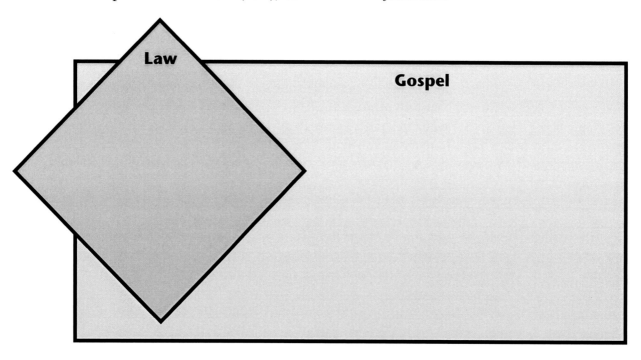

Law

Gospel

The Prophetic Scriptures

Like a worker who posts road signs, biblical prophets had the job of sharing messages.

The prophet forth told by proclaiming what was happening at that time. The prophet foretold by telling others about what would happen in the future.

The messages the prophets shared were not their own interpretations of events or predictions about the future. God called His prophets to share His words of warning, of judgment, of direction, and of promise.

Determine whether each of the Old Testament passages found in the chart below shares a message of forth telling, foretelling, or both. Then determine whether the passage proclaims God's judgment on His people, offers them His promise, or both. Mark the columns to indicate your answers.

Messages from God's Prophets	Forth Telling	Foretelling	Judgment	Promise
1. "Your country lies desolate; your cities are burned with fire; in your very presence foreigners devour your land; it is desolate, as overthrown by foreigners" (Isaiah 1:7).				
2. "And I will restore your judges as at first, and your counselors as at the beginning. Afterward you shall be called the city of righteousness, the faithful city" (Isaiah 1:26).				
3. "Therefore the Lord Himself will give you a sign. Behold, the virgin shall conceive and bear a Son, and shall call His name Immanuel" (Isaiah 7:14).				
4. " 'Do not be afraid of them, for I am with you to deliver you,' declares the Lord" (Jeremiah 1:8).				
5. "Flee! Save yourselves! You will be like a juniper in the desert! For, because you trusted in your works and your treasures, you also shall be taken" (Jeremiah 48:6–7).				
6. "But you, O Bethlehem Ephrathah, who are too little to be among the clans of Judah, from you shall come forth for Me one who is to be ruler in Israel, whose coming forth is from of old, from ancient days" (Micah 5:2).				
7. "Thus says the Lord God: Disaster after disaster! Behold, it comes" (Ezekiel 7:5).				
8. "Their Redeemer is strong; the Lord of hosts is His name. He will surely plead their cause, that He may give rest to the earth" (Jeremiah 50:34).				

Selected Old Testament Prophecies of the Messiah

The Gift That Lasts a Lifetime

1. What gift is shown in this picture?

2. Is this a gift that everyone can use? Why or why not?

3. Who gives us this gift?

4. How can we be sure the gift will last for the rest of our lives?

God's Plan of Salvation: Prophecy and Fulfillment

In the Bible, God reveals His plan for our salvation throughout the Old and New Testaments. Both testaments teach God's Law: how God wants us to live and how we fail to live as He commands. Both testaments also teach us the Gospel message: how God forgives our sin and gives us eternal life.

In the Old Testament, God often spoke His Gospel message through messianic prophecies. Gospel messages in the New Testament often tell about how Jesus fulfilled the Old Testament prophecies.

Inside the twelve small boxes on the next page are references from the Old Testament that record messianic prophecies. The New Testament references in the outer ring of large boxes tell how Jesus fulfilled those prophecies.

Complete the page by doing the following:

- Read each New Testament passage, then write or sketch what it tells about Jesus.
- Read each Old Testament prophecy and determine which ones are fulfilled by which New Testament passage. Then write in the smaller corner box of each the letter above the New Testament reference.
- Color the boxes that tell about Jesus' suffering and death.
- In the lines at the bottom of the page, write the letters in the order they appear in the corners from left to right, top to bottom. What do these words remind you about the Bible?

10

R
Matthew 1:22–23

N
Luke 23:36

H
Acts 2:31–32

D
Matthew 26:33–34; 27:30–31

R
Matthew 21:4–9

Malachi 3:1	Psalm 41:9	Isaiah 7:14
Isaiah 53:3	Psalm 22:1	Psalm 69:21
Micah 5:2	Zechariah 12:10	Zechariah 9:9–13
Isaiah 35:5–6	Jonah 1:17	Psalm 16:9–10

D
Luke 2:4–7

W
Matthew 11:10

O
John 13:18, 26

A
Matthew 27:46

T
Matthew 12:40

T
John 19:34–37

U
John 5:6–8; 9:6–7

Isaiah's Words of Law and Gospel

The Prophet Isaiah

The prophet Isaiah wrote the book of the Bible titled Isaiah during a stormy period in the history of God's people. Isaiah's story begins as the long reign of King Uzziah ends (740 BC). Under Uzziah's direction, Judah had become a strong and important country due to a mighty army and increased trade. Now Judah's enemies are gathered at her borders and plot her destruction. This is the setting for God's call to Isaiah. Read about the prophet's call in Isaiah 6:1–13.

1. Where was Isaiah when the Lord called him (verse 1)?

2. What did Isaiah see (verses 1–2)?

3. How did Isaiah feel in the presence of God (verse 5)?

4. Why did the angel put the burning coal to Isaiah's lips (verse 7)?

5. What did God want Isaiah to do (verses 8–9)?

6. How did Isaiah feel about becoming God's prophet (verse 8)?

Did You Know? The name *Isaiah* means "the LORD saves."

Prophecies Proclaimed

Isaiah obediently delivered God's message to the people in Judah.

7. What was Isaiah's message? How was the prophet's message received (Isaiah 22:12–13)?

God's people did not repent. They continued in their idolatry and wickedness. After years of prophetic warnings, God's judgment fell with a vengeance upon Judah. But God remembered His remnant—those few who remained faithful to the Lord even through years of exile as foreign slaves.

8. What message of hope did Isaiah prophesy to the faithful remnant (Isaiah 54:7)?

The Apocalyptic Scriptures

Our word *apocalypse* comes from the Greek word meaning "revelation." In biblical terms, apocalyptic literature has to do with something revealed. This type of writing can be hard to understand. The people who wrote in this style experienced visions or dreams in which God revealed something special to them. These revelations often talk about the end of the world. There are a lot of symbols, such as animals, objects, or numbers, which stand for other things. Examples of apocalyptic literature in the Old Testament are found in books like Ezekiel and Daniel. In the New Testament, we have the Book of Revelation.

Martin Luther wrote this about the Book of Revelation: "We can profit by this book and make good use of it . . . for our comfort! We can rest assured that neither force nor lies, neither wisdom nor holiness, neither tribulation nor suffering shall suppress Christendom [the Christian Church], but it will gain the victory and conquer at last" (Luther's Works, 35:409).

Ezekiel

God's Watchman

Ezekiel's Call and Vision

1. As the vision approaches, what does Ezekiel see (Ezekiel 1:4)?

2. Briefly describe the cherubim or attendants to the throne pictured in 1:5–14.

3. The likeness of the glory of the Lord is described in 1:26–28. Tell about it in your own words.

4. How does God describe His people (2:3–5; 3:7)?

5. Summarize the call of Ezekiel (2:1–3:15). What job does God give His prophet? How does God reassure Ezekiel?

Ezekiel—God's Watchman

6. Describe Ezekiel's role as watchman as presented in 3:16–21.

7. Whom does God hold responsible for sin (3:18)?

8. Who will empower Ezekiel to prophesy (3:24–27)?

9. Read 5:1–17. Briefly summarize Ezekiel's prophetic actions and their meaning for Jerusalem.

10. What purpose will Jerusalem's destruction serve for the surrounding nations (5:14–15)?

The Wrath of Judgment

11. What will God do to the idolatrous high places and idol worshipers (6:4–7)?

12. What will be the response of those who escape (6:8–10)?

13. Ezekiel 6:11–12 describes the three different methods by which judgment will come. Name them.

14. Once God's judgment is complete, what will the people once again realize (6:10, 13–14)?

15. What significant event occurs in 10:1–22?

Ezekiel Proclaims God's Mercy

16. The exiles were driven from Jerusalem, far away from the sanctuary of the Lord's temple. According to 11:16, where can the scattered people find sanctuary in exile?

17. Read 11:17 to discover God's merciful plan for His faithful remnant.

18. According to 11:18, how will the returning remnant demonstrate their faithfulness to the one true God?

19. What does God plan to do for His faithful remnant (11:19)?

20. According to 11:20, what will God's action enable His people to do?

Revelation 4–22

Revelation Reflections

Use the following questions to help you apply John's Revelation to your life.

Scene I—The Throne Room of God

1. Consider Romans 6:23 and 1 Corinthians 15:17. Then explain why John wept at the suspense over who was able to open the scroll (Revelation 5:4–5).

2. What is the result of Jesus' opening of the scroll (Revelation 5:9–10)?

3. Review the past twenty-four hours. Think about times you have broken God's commands, disobeying God and disappointing and harming others by your thoughts, words, and actions. Write a sentence telling what Jesus' opening of the scroll means to you.

Scene II—The Seven Seals

1. Those who are residents of heaven are those possessing the gift of faith in Jesus, God's Son and the Savior of the world. According to Revelation 7:9–10:

   a. How many residents of heaven are there?

   b. From where have they come?

2. Why are their robes white (Revelation 7:14)?

3. Describe their life in heaven (Revelation 7:15–17).

Scenes III, IV, and V—Life in the Last Days

1. These scenes describe the persecution and hardships we, the people of God, will endure as we live in a world under the fallen condition and control of Satan. Having conquered sin, death, and the power of the devil, why does God allow this evil world to continue (Matthew 24:14)?

2. See 1 Peter 1:3–9. What power keeps us in the faith in the face of trials and sufferings, even as it enables us to share the Good News with those who do not yet believe (verse 5)?

Scene VI—The Final Gathering

1. Describe the special relationship we will one day enjoy with God (Revelation 21:3–7).

2. Write the final promise of Jesus to us recorded in John's Revelation—the last words of Jesus we find in the Bible (Revelation 22:20).

Poetic Books

Poetic books of the Bible express the depth of human emotions. Also referred to as Wisdom Literature, the poetic books of Job, Psalms, Proverbs, Ecclesiastes, and Song of Solomon use poetic techniques that differ from those associated with traditional English poetry. Instead of relying on rhyme and meter, Hebrew poetry uses figures of speech, repetition, and saying the same thing in other ways to express meaning and make a point.

Chief among the meanings conveyed by Wisdom Literature are human struggles against evil, the devastating consequences of sin, and God's protecting, sustaining, and forgiving love. King David knew each of these subjects well. Throughout his life, he wrote and sang songs to the Lord about things happening in his life and thanked and praised God for His great goodness. You can read some of these songs—called psalms—in the Book of Psalms in the Bible.

David wrote a number of different types of psalms. Three examples follow. Read the description of each type of psalm and then use the letters *a*, *b*, or *c* to classify each Bible reference.

Type of Psalms

a. Praise—a psalm of worship and praise, confessing God's knowledge and power.
b. Prophecy—a psalm describing God's plan for the future.
c. lament—a psalm expressing sorrow and the need for God's rescue.

Psalm Reference

_____ 1. Psalm 22:1–11
_____ 2. Psalm 8
_____ 3. Psalm 110
_____ 4. Psalm 64
_____ 5. Psalm 40:1–5

God Speaks His Love for Us through the Psalms

God continues to support and encourage His people through the psalms. Below are some possible situations you might face. Choose a psalm verse that speaks to each and write its letter before the situation. There may be more than one answer for each.

_____ 1. When I feel alone or overwhelmed by stress
_____ 2. When I am sick or afraid of death
_____ 3. When I am afraid someone is going to hurt me
_____ 4. When I have trouble obeying
_____ 5. When I feel overcome by the burden of sin

a. "The Lord is a stronghold for the oppressed, a stronghold in times of trouble." Psalm 9:9
b. "Even though I walk through the valley of the shadow of death, I will fear no evil, for You are with me; Your rod and Your staff, they comfort me." Psalm 23:4
c. "The Lord is my light and my salvation; whom shall I fear? The Lord is the stronghold of my life; of whom shall I be afraid?" Psalm 27:1
d. "The Lord is near to the brokenhearted and saves the crushed in spirit." Psalm 34:18
e. "Those who trust in the Lord are like Mount Zion, which cannot be moved, but abides forever." Psalm 125:1
f. "The Lord is gracious and merciful, slow to anger and abounding in steadfast love. The Lord is good to all, and His mercy is over all that He has made." Psalm 145:8–9

The Poetic Proverbs

The Old Testament book Proverbs uses the following three writing styles to impart godly wisdom.

    A. Lines of similar or parallel ideas in a two-line repetition. Example: *A good name is to be chosen rather than great riches, and favor is better than silver or gold.* (Proverbs 22:1)

    B. Contrasting statements in two lines. Example: *A soft answer turns away wrath, but a harsh word stirs up anger.* (Proverbs 15:1)

    C. An observation about nature from which we can learn. Example: *Go to the ant, O sluggard; consider her ways, and be wise. Without having any chief, officer, or ruler, she prepares her bread in summer and gathers her food in harvest.* (Proverbs 6:6–8)

What wisdom has God given you in His Word? Communicate some of this wisdom in your own words, using each of the styles found in the Book of Proverbs.

Style A:

Style B:

Style C:

Narratives in God's Word

The narrative style of writing is used to tell stories. The New Testament books of Matthew, Mark, Luke, and John, referred to as the Gospels, tell about the birth, life, death, and resurrection of Jesus, God's Son and the Savior of the world. The chart below compares these four great books.

Gospel	Author	Date & Place of Writing	Audience	Purpose
Matthew	Matthew, one of the 12 apostles	Late AD 50s to 70s in Palestine or Syrian Antioch	Jewish people	Prove to the Jewish leaders that Jesus is the Messiah, the promised King of the Jews.
Mark	John Mark, a close friend of Peter	AD 50–70 in Ephesus or possibly in Jerusalem	Romans	Present the action-packed account of Jesus, the powerful Savior/Teacher/Servant; prepare Christian readers for suffering and persecution.
Luke	Luke, a physician and companion of Paul	Probably written in Rome, but possibly Ephesus or Caesarea in AD 60–80	Greeks	Show Jesus as the Son of God but also true man who came to save the whole world.
John	John, one of the 12 disciples, "the disciple whom Jesus loved"	AD 50–90 in Ephesus or possibly in Jerusalem	All people	Build up and win new converts to Jesus, who was God made man, their personal Savior.

1. Read John 20:31. Why were the Gospels written?

2. Let's take a quick look at the beginning of each of the Gospels.

    a. Scan Matthew 1:1–17. Considering the original audience and purpose of Matthew, why is the genealogy of Jesus so important (see especially verse 1)?

    b. Why is it not important for Mark to contain a genealogy?

    c. Scan the genealogy included by Luke toward the beginning of his Gospel (Luke 3:21–38, especially verse 38). To whom does Luke trace the ancestry of Jesus and why do you think he did so?

    d. See John 1:1. Explain John's message about Jesus, here referred to as the Word.

Matthew's Narrative

Matthew's Gospel begins with an account of Jesus' birth and ends with the account of His passion, death, and resurrection. Five sections are arranged between these accounts that contain Jesus' deeds and then Jesus' words. Summarize the words and actions in each of the five sections.

First section: Matthew 3:1–7:29

a. Deeds: 3:1–4:25

b. Words: 5:1–7:29

Second section: Matthew 8:1–11:1

a. Deeds: 8:1–9:35

b. Words: 9:36–11:1

Third section: Matthew 11:2–13:53

a. Deeds: 11:2–12:50

b. Words: 13:1–53

Fourth section: Matthew 13:54–18:35

a. Deeds: 13:54–17:27

b. Words: 18:1–35

Fifth section: Matthew 19:1–25:46

a. Deeds: 19:1–22:46

b. Words: 23:1–25:46

Mark's Narrative

Mark's Gospel tells about Jesus' life and work in a concise way. But who is Mark, also called John or John Mark? Match each of the following Bible selections with corresponding statements about John, also called Mark.

_____ 1. Because he referred to Mark as his son, some think Peter may have led Mark to faith in Jesus.

_____ 2. Mark and Luke worked together with the apostle Paul.

_____ 3. Paul said Mark was helpful to him in his work of spreading the Gospel.

_____ 4. Mark was the cause of a bitter disagreement between Paul and Barnabas because Mark at one point had deserted the missionaries.

_____ 5. Mark accompanied Paul and Barnabas on the return from Paul's first missionary journey.

_____ 6. Mark's mother, Mary, had a large home where many Christians met and prayed, and to which Peter came after his miraculous release from prison.

_____ 7. Mark was a cousin of Barnabas, Paul's co-worker and fellow evangelist.

a. "When Peter came to himself, he said, 'Now I am sure that the Lord has sent His angel and rescued me from the hand of Herod and from all that the Jewish people were expecting.' When he realized this, he went to the house of Mary, the mother of John whose other name was Mark, where many were gathered together and were praying." Acts 12:11–12

b. "But the word of God increased and multiplied. And Barnabas and Saul [Paul] returned from Jerusalem when they had completed their service, bringing with them John, whose other name was Mark." Acts 12:24–25

c. "Aristarchus my fellow prisoner greets you, and Mark the cousin of Barnabas." Colossians 4:10

d. "And after some days Paul said to Barnabas, 'Let us return and visit the brothers in every city where we proclaimed the word of the Lord, and see how they are.' Now Barnabas wanted to take with them John called Mark. But Paul thought best not to take with them one who had withdrawn from them in Pamphylia and had not gone with them to the work. And there arose a sharp disagreement, so that they separated from each other. Barnabas took Mark with him and sailed away to Cyprus." Acts 15:36–39

e. [Paul wrote,] "Get Mark and bring him with you, for he is very useful to me for ministry." 2 Timothy 4:11

f. [Paul wrote,] "Epaphras, my fellow prisoner in Christ Jesus, sends greetings to you, and so do Mark, Aristarchus, Demas, and Luke, my fellow workers." Philemon 1:23–24

g. [Peter wrote,] "She who is at Babylon, who is likewise chosen, sends you greetings, and so does, Mark, my son." 1 Peter 5:13

Luke's Narrative

Luke, the author of the Gospel that bears his name, was a physician. Luke's Gospel gives special emphasis to the healing provided through Jesus, our Savior. Luke's Gospel also records for us more of our Lord's prayers than any other Gospel.

Read each of the following references from Luke that tell of Jesus talking to God in prayer. Record any pertinent information about the occasion, setting, or content of Jesus' prayers.

1. Luke 3:21

2. Luke 5:15–16

3. Luke 6:12–13

4. Luke 9:10–17

5. Luke 9:18

6. Luke 9:28–29

7. Luke 10:21–22

8. Luke 11:1–4

9. Luke 22:14–20

10. Luke 22:32

11. Luke 22:39–46

12. Luke 23:33–34

13. Luke 24:30

John's Narrative

From Darkness to Light

Often when we enter a dark room, we are blind—our eyes do not receive enough light to enable us to see. Similarly, the eyes of a blind person do not receive light. God's Word refers to sin as darkness. Those living in sin are spiritually blind. God sent the Light into the world to eliminate spiritual blindness.

Read the following references from John's Gospel. Match the beginning of each passage with its concluding portion as you find it in the column on the right. Then state in your own words the message of each about spiritual darkness or light, blindness or sight.

_____ 1. John 1:4–5: "In [Jesus] was life, and the life was the light of men. The light shines in the darkness,

_____ 2. John 3:3: "Jesus answered him, 'Truly, truly, I say to you, unless one is born again

_____ 3. John 3:16, 19: "For God so loved the world, that He gave His only Son, that whoever believes in Him should not perish but have eternal life. . . . And this is the judgment: the light has come into the world,

_____ 4. John 8:12: "Again Jesus spoke to them, saying, 'I am the light of the world. Whoever follows Me will not walk in darkness,

_____ 5. John 12:35: "So Jesus said to them, 'The light is among you for a little while longer. Walk while you have the light,

_____ 6. John 12:36: "While you have the light, believe in the light,

_____ 7. John 12:46: "[Jesus said,] 'I have come into the world as light,

a. lest darkness overtake you. The one who walks in the darkness does not know where he is going.'"

b. that you may become sons of light."

c. so that whoever believes in Me may not remain in darkness.'"

d. he cannot see the kingdom of God.'"

e. and people loved the darkness rather than the light because their works were evil."

f. and the darkness has not overcome it."

g. but will have the light of life.'"

A Bible Concordance

A concordance is a book or part of a book that lists common words from the Bible. A concordance gives a portion of each verse containing the word and the reference for the verse.

```
TEACHING
Pr      1: 8   forsake not your mother's t.
Pr      6:23   is a lamp and the t a light
Mt   15: 9   t as doctrines the commandments
Mt   28:20   t them to observe all that I
Jn      7:17   he will know whether the t
Ac      2:42   apostles' t and the fellowship,
Ac   15: 1   and were t the brothers
Ro      6:17   t to which you were committed,
Ro   12: 7   one who teaches, in his t;
Col   1:28   warning everyone and t
Col   3:16   t and admonishing one.
1Ti   4:13   to exhortation, to t.
1Ti   5:17   labor in preaching and t.
1Ti   6: 3   and the t that accords with,
2Ti   3:16   by God and profitable for t,
2Ti   4: 3   people will not endure sound t
Ti      2: 7   and in your t show integrity,
2Jn   1: 9   Whoever abides in the t has
```

A concordance doesn't usually define a word like a Bible dictionary does, but it does provide an easy way to find out where in the Bible a word occurs. Included above is a section of a concordance to which we might go to find Bible passages that contain the word *teaching*. Use this example of a Bible concordance to answer the questions included below.

1. What Bible reference connects teaching with light?

2. Which Bible verse makes reference to a mother's teaching?

3. What Bible reference deals with showing integrity in teaching?

4. What Bible verse refers to both preaching and teaching?

5. What Bible passage talks about the apostles' teaching?

6. What Bible passage deals with the concept of sound teaching?

7. What Bible verse talks about teaching the brothers?

The Right Word for a Concordance Search

Directions: Circle a key word in the passage. Find the key word on the accompanying concordance page; note the Bible reference and find it in your Bible (ESV). Fill in the words that are missing in each passage. Provide the Bible reference inside each set of parentheses.

Hint: Be sure to look at the words at the top of the concordance page to identify the first (left) and last (right) key word found on the concordance page.

1. If you _____ Him, He will be found.

   (_____)

2. We too were found to be _____.

   (_____)

3. _____, the founder and _____ of our faith,

   who for the _____ that was set before Him endured the cross, despising the

   _____, and is seated at the right hand of the _____ of God.

   (_____)

4. Keep your life free from the love of _____, and be _____

   with what you have, for [the Lord] has said, "I will never leave you nor

   _____ you. (_____)

5. So if the _____ sets you free, you will be free indeed.

   (_____)

6. The _____ sets the _____ free.

   (_____)

7. _____ loved us and gave Himself up for us, a fragrant _____

   and _____ to God.

   (_____)

Found

FOUND

2Ch	15: 2	you seek Him, He will be *f*.
Pr	10:13	who has understanding, wisdom is *f*,
Ps	32: 6	at a time when You may be *f*
Is	55: 6	The Lord while He my be *f*,
Da	5:27	in the balances and *f* wanting.
Lk	15:24	he was lost, and is *f*."
Gal	2:17	we too were *f* to be sinners,
Php	2: 8	And being *f* in human form,
2Pt	1:20	be diligent to be *f* by Him

FOUNDATION

Isa	28: 6	cornerstone, a sure *f*;
Mt	25:34	for you from the *f* of the world.
Lk	11:50	shed from the *f* of the world,
Jn	17:24	You loved Me before the *f* of the world
1Co	3:11	For no one can lay a *f*
Eph	2:20	built on the *f* of the apostles
2Ti	2:19	But God's *f* stands,
1Pt	1:20	was foreknown before the *f*

FOUNDATIONS (FOUNDATION)

Is	28:16	the *f* of many generations

FOUNDER

Heb	2:10	*f* of their salvation
Heb	12: 2	Jesus, the *f* and perfecter

FOUNTAIN

Jer	2:13	the *f* of living waters,
Jer	9: 1	and my eyes a *f* of tears,
Zec	13: 1	there shall be a *f* opened

FOXES

Mt	8:20	And Jesus said, to him, "F

FRAGRANCE

2Co	2:14	*f* of the knowledge of Him
2Co	2:16	*f* from life to life.

Friend

FRAGRANT

Eph	5: 2	Himself up for us, as a *f* offering

FREE (FREED FREEDOM FREELY)

Ps	110: 3	offer themselves *f* on that day.
Ps	146: 7	The Lord sets prisoners *f*;
Is	58: 6	to let the oppressed go *f*,
Jn	8:32	and the truth will set you *f*."
Jn	8:36	sets you *f*, you will be *f* indeed.
Ro	5:17	and the *f* gift of righteousness
Ro	8: 2	the Spirit of life has set you *f*
Gal	2: 4	our *f* that we have in Christ Jesus,
Gal	3:28	there is neither slave nor *f*,
Gal	5: 1	*f* Christ has set us *f*.
Gal	5:16	For you were called to *f*
Heb	13: 5	your life *f* from love of money,
1Pe	2:16	are *f* not using your *f*
Rev	1: 5	To Him who loves us and has *f*,

FRET

Ps	37: 1	*F* not yourself because of evildoers

FRIEND (FRIENDS FRIENDSHIP)

Ex	33:11	as a man speaks to his *f*.
Pr	17:17	A *f* loves at all times,
Pr	18:24	there is a *f* that sticks closer than a brother
Pr	25:14	The *f* of the Lord is for those
Pr	27: 6	are the wounds or a *f*
Pr	27:10	Do not forsake your *f* and
Jn	15:13	lay down his life for his *f*.
Jn	15:14	You are My *f* if you do what
Jn	15:15	but I have called you *f*, for

Concordance Bible Study

Use the page, "A Section from a Concordance," to answers these questions.

1. The concordance contains both noun and verb forms of the word *redeem*. To *redeem* means "to ransom or buy back, as to purchase freedom for a slave."
   a. Give the earliest Bible reference dealing with the redeem/redemption concept.

   b. See verse 1 of the chapter of the Bible containing the first reference to the redeem/redemption concept.

      1. Who has redeemed God's people?

      2. Who are the people of God that have been redeemed?

2. According to the concordance, one chapter in the Old Testament provides two entries for the word *redeemer*.
   a. Give these two references.

   b. According to the first of these references, what is the name of this redeemer?

3. According to the two entries found in Paul's letter to the Galatians,
   a. from what has Christ redeemed us?

   b. how did Christ redeem us?

   c. what did Christ's redemption provide for us?

4. According to Isaiah 44:22, how would God have us respond to the redemption He has provided?

5. Look up the verse in which Luke first uses the word *redeemed*. Name the person who is speaking in this verse about the redemption God provided.

A Section from a Concordance

REDEEM

Ex	6: 6	and I will *r* you with an
Ps	25: 22	*R* Israel, O God,
Ps	31: 5	*r* me, O LORD
Ps	44: 26	*R* us for the sake of Your
Ps	69: 18	Draw near to my soul *r* me;
Ps	119:134	*R* me from man's
Is	50: 2	shortened, that it cannot *r*
Hos	13: 14	Shall I *r* them from Death?
Mi	4: 10	there the LORD will *r* you
Gal	4: 5	to *r* those under law,
Ti	2: 14	to *r* us from all lawlessness

REDEEMED

Ex	15: 13	People whom You have *r*
Dt	7: 8	*r* you from the house of slavery,
Ps	107: 2	Let the *r* of the LORD say so
Is	43: 1	"Fear not, for I have *r* you:
Is	44: 22	return to Me, for I have *r* you.
Is	52: 3	and you shall be *r* without
Is	52: 9	people; He has *r* Jerusalem
Jer	31: 11	and has *r* him from hands
Lm	3: 58	O Lord; You have *r* my life.
Lk	1: 68	for He has visited and *r* His
Gal	3: 13	Christ *r* us from the curse

REDEEMER

Job	19: 25	For I know that my *R* lives,
Ps	19: 14	O LORD, my rock and my *r*.
Is	41: 14	your *R*, is the Holy One
Is	44: 6	the King of Israel and His *R*,
Is	47: 4	Our *R*—the LORD of hosts is
Is	54: 5	Holy One of Israel is your *R*,
Is	54: 8	says the LORD, your *R*.
Is	63: 16	Our *R* from of old is Your name.

REDEEMS

Ps	34: 22	The LORD *r* the life of His
Ps	55: 18	He *r* my soul is safety from
Ps	72: 14	and violence He *r* their life,
Ps	103: 4	who *r* my life from the pit,
Heb	9: 15	that *r* them from the

REDEMPTION

Ex	21: 30	then he shall give for the *r*
Ru	4: 6	Take my right of *r* yourself,
Ps	111: 9	He sent *r* to His people; He
Ps	130: 7	with Him is plentiful *r*.
Lk	2: 38	for the *r* of Jerusalem.
Lk	21: 28	because your *r* is drawing
Ro	3: 24	through the *r* that is in
Rm	8: 23	as sons, the *r* of our bodies.
1Co	1: 30	and sanctification through *r*,
Eph	1: 7	In Him we have *r* through His blood
	4: 30	were sealed for the day of *r*.
Col	1: 14	in whom we have *r*, the forgiveness
Heb	9: 12	thus securing an eternal *r*.

Using a Concordance

Consider the concordance entry for the word *Commandments*, reproduced for you below. Comparing concordances, you will note that concordances differ in placement of Bible references. This sample places the Bible references on the right of the Bible words.

This activity gets you into the use of the concordance for a specific topical purpose. The challenge activity directs you to work on your own to expand your knowledge of a specific commandment.

Commandments	
who love Me and keep My *c.*	Ex 20: 6
of the covenant—the Ten C.	Ex 34:28
These *c* that I give you today are	Dt 6: 6
who love Him and keep His *c.*	Dt 7: 9
Keep the *c* of the LORD your God	Dt 8: 6
if you obey the *c* the LORD	Dt 11:27
Fear God and keep His *c,*	Ecc 12:13
one of the least of these *c,*	Mt 5:19
as doctrines the *c* of men."	Mt 15: 9
you would enter life, keep the *c*	Mt 19: 7
on these two *c* depend all."	Mt 22:40
but keeping the *c* of God	1Co 7:19
know Him, if we keep His *c.*	1Jn 2: 3
And His *c* are not burdensome	1Jn 5: 3
on those who keep the *c* of God	Rev 12:17

1. Look up the verses in the concordance entries given here. Put a star by the verse that helps you understand the importance of fearing God and keeping the commandments.

2. Put a cross by the verses that help you understand that the commandments are not a burden for those who love and trust in Jesus.

3. What new ideas or understandings do you have from this study? Record them here.

Challenge: Think of other key words in any of the Ten Commandments. Use them to do additional concordance work.

John 10:11—Cross References and Notes

John 10:11 in *The Lutheran Study Bible* looks like this:
11 k I am the good shepherd. The good shepherd l lays down His life for the sheep.

In the margin near the words of John 10:11, you will find the following cross references.
11 kIsa 40:11; Eze 34:12, 23; 37:24; Zec 13:7; Heb 13:20; 1Pt 2:25; 5:4; [ch 21:15–17; Ps 23; Rev 7:17] lvv 15, 17; ch 15:13; 1Jn 3:16 [Mt 20:28; Mk 10:45]

Note that the references following k indicate other places where God is referred to as the Good Shepherd. Those following l give other places speaking about the shepherd sacrificing Himself in order to save the sheep. Look up five of these references and tell what additional information or insights can be learned from each.

Reference   Insights or Information

_____   _____
                     _____

_____   _____
                     _____

_____   _____
                     _____

_____   _____
                     _____

_____   _____
                     _____

Study Bibles also include notes on the bottom of the page. These notes further help the reader understand, apply, or meditate on aspects of the verse identified. Following is the note in *The Lutheran Study Bible* relating to John 10:11. *Luth* is short for Martin Luther *AE* refers to the American Edition of Luther's Works. The volume and page number are also indicated.

10:11 *I am.* See pp 1784–85. *good shepherd.* Luth: "In this single little word 'shepherd' there are gathered together in one almost all the good and comforting things that we praise in God" (AE 12:152). *lays down His life for the sheep.* Jesus did not risk His life for the sheep merely to set a noble example; He gave His life as an atoning sacrifice for them. See note 1:29.

What thoughts provided in this note are especially meaningful to you today?

Cross-Reference Work
The Ten Commandments

Look at the cross-reference section to the Ten Commandments in a Bible that contains margin references (see Exodus 20:1–17). These references help you expand your understanding of the commandment as well as show how Jesus used the commandment in His teaching.

1. Select one commandment and write it in your own words.

2. List here other Bible references to this commandment. Look up each reference. In the space provided, write the new information or insights these verses add. If there is a New Testament reference, find the context of how Jesus used this commandment in His teaching.

3. If Jesus used this commandment directly in His teaching, record the use here.

4. Finish the following statement: From my study, I believe that this commandment means . . .

Background to the Book of 2 John

Consider the following as it might appear as an introduction to the Book of 2 John. Answer the questions that follow.

Author: John the apostle
Date: AD 85–95
Theme and Purpose
This Epistle is the only book in the Bible addressed to a woman. It stresses the related themes of truth and love. Genuine truth and love are found only in Jesus Christ.
During the early years of Christianity, evangelists and teachers traveled from place to place sharing the Gospel. Christians regularly welcomed these missionaries into their homes and assisted them in their work. But false teachers also sought the hospitality and support of believers. In this letter, John warns against unintentionally supporting and assisting teachings that detract from or deny the truth.

Outline

Greeting (verses 1–3)
Truth and love (verses 4–6)
False teachers (verses 7–11)
Conclusion (verses 12–13)

Information about 2 John

1. How many verses does the Book of 2 John contain?

2. What is unique about this book?

3. Who wrote it and when was it written?

4. What two themes can be found in the Book of 2 John?

5. What warning does John offer the faithful in this book?

A Brief Study of a Book of the Bible

Read 2 John. Then study the book briefly using the questions that follow.

2 John

[1a]The elder to the elect lady and her children, [b]whom I love in the truth, and not only I, but also all who [c]know [d]the truth,[2e]because of the truth that abides in us and will be with us forever:

[3f]Grace, mercy, and peace will be with us, from God the Father and from Jesus Christ, the Father's Son, in truth and love.

[4g]I rejoiced greatly to find some of your children walking in the truth, just as we were commanded by the Father. [5]And now I ask you, dear lady—[h]not as though I were writing you a new commandment, but the one we have had from the beginning—[i]that we love one another. [6]And [j]this is love, that we walk according to His commandments; this is the commandment, just [k]as you have heard from the beginning, so that you should walk in it. [7]For [l]many deceivers [m]have gone out into the world, [n]those who do not confess the

AD 85-95

1 [a]3Jn 1; [1Pt 5:1] [b]1Jn 3:18; 3Jn 1 [c]Jn8:32; [1Tim2:4; Heb 10:26] [d]Jn 1:17; 14:6; S Gal 2:5
2 [e][1Co 13:6]
3 [f]S 1Ti 1:2; 2Tm 1:2; [Jude 2]
4 [g]3Jn 3, 4
5 [h]1Jn 2:7 [i]S 1Jn 3:11
6 [i]1Jn 5:3; [1Jn 2:5]; S Jn 14:15 [k]1Jn 2:24
7 [l][Mt 24:5, 24; 2Pt2:1]; S 1Jn2:18, 26 [M]1Jn 4:1 [n]1Jn 2:22; 4:2, 3
8 [o][Gal 3:4; Heb 10:35] [P][Gal 4:11] [q]S 1Co 3:8
9 [r]S 1Jn 2:22 [s]S 1Jn 2:23
10 [t][Rm 16:17; Gal 1:8, 9; 2Th 3:6, 14; Ti 3:10]
11 [u][1Tm 5:22]
12 [v]3Jn 13 [w]3Jn 14 [x]Jn 15:11; 17:13

coming of Jesus Christ in the flesh. Such a one is the deceiver and the antichrist. [8]Watch yourselves, [o]so that you may not [p]lose what we have worked for, but that you [q]may win a full reward. [9]Everyone who goes on ahead and does not [r]abide in the teaching of Christ, [s]does not have God. Whoever abides in the teaching [s]has both the Father and the Son. [10]If anyone comes to you and does not bring this teaching, [t]do not receive him into your house or give him any greeting, [11]for whoever greets him [u]takes part in his wicked works.

[12] [v]Though I have much to write to you, I would rather not to use paper and ink. [w]Instead I hope to come to you and talk face to face, [x]so that our joy may be complete.

[13]The children of your elect sister greet you.

---

1 *elder.* John may have served as an elder in the church, perhaps the church at Ephesus. *elect lady.* A follower of Jesus or perhaps a figurative designation for the members of a congregation. *her children.* Children of the woman or perhaps members of the local congregation.

7–11 *deceivers.* Most likely a reference to Gnostics who believed and taught that God's Son did not really become flesh but rather only temporarily came upon a man named Jesus between the time of His Baptism and His crucifixion. *antichrist.* One of the enemies of Christ foretold to appear before Christ's second coming.

13 *elect sister.* A reference either to another Christian woman or perhaps a designation for another congregation.

---

1. John addresses this letter to the elect lady and her children. What two possible identities might be represented in this address?

2. Circle the word *truth* every time it appears in 2 John. How many times does the word *truth* occur in the letter?

3. Circle the word *love* every time it appears in 2 John. How many times does the word *love* occur in the letter?

4. According to verse 6, how do the followers of Jesus show their love for Him?

5. John warns against deceptive teachings (verses 7–11). Gnosticism was a chief heresy in John's day.
   a. According to the verse notes, what did Gnostics believe?

   b. What words in verse 7 suggest that John was thinking of the Gnostics when he warned about deceivers?

6. According to the reference identified by the letter following the phrase teaching of Christ in verse 9, what benefits are associated with those who continue in Jesus' teaching?

7. What two things in this epistle does John associate with joy (verses 4 and 12)?

Using the Best Reference

When we need to get more ideas, solve a problem, or answer a question using God's Word, we have a choice of resources. To the right are examples of Bible study helps from a study Bible. Look at the questions below. Then choose the best resource to answer each question. After you have picked the resource, go ahead and use it to answer the question.

1. What two bodies of water are connected by the Jordan River?

   Resource:

   Answer:

2. Why did Jesus need to be baptized?

   Resource:

   Answer:

3. What kind of Baptism was John's Baptism? Support this answer with a reference from God's Word.

   Resource:

   Answer:

4. What towns are near the Jordan River?

   Resource:

   Answer:

5. Why did the Holy Spirit come onto Jesus?

   Resource:

   Answer:

Map

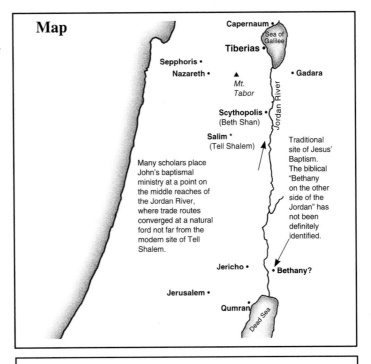

Many scholars place John's baptismal ministry at a point on the middle reaches of the Jordan River, where trade routes converged at a natural ford not far from the modern site of Tell Shalem.

Traditional site of Jesus' Baptism. The biblical "Bethany on the other side of the Jordan" has not been definitely identified.

Study Notes for Matthew 3

3:13 ˢS Mt 3:1; S Mk 1:4 **3:16** ᵗEze 1:1; Jn 1:51; Ac 7:56; 10:11; Rev 4:1; 19:11 ᵘIs 11:2; 42:1 **3:17** ᵛDt 4:12; Mt 17:5; Jn 12:28 ʷPs 2:7; Ac 13:33; Heb 1:1-5; 5:5; 2Pe 1:17, 18 ˣIs 42:1; Mt 12:18; 17:5; Mk 1:11; 9:7; Lk 3:22; 9:35; 2Pe 1:17

3:15 This occasion marked the beginning of Christ's Messianic ministry. There were several reasons for His Baptism: 1. The first, mentioned here, was "to fulfill all righteousness." The Baptism indicated that He was consecrated to God and officially approved by Him, as especially shown in the descent of the Holy Spirit (v. 16) and the words of the Father (v. 17; cf. Ps 2:7; Is 42:1). All God's righteous requirements for the Messiah were fully met in Jesus. 2. At Jesus' Baptism John publicly announced the arrival of the Messiah and the inception of His ministry (Jn 1:31–34). 3. By His Baptism, Jesus completely identified Himself with man's sin and failure (though He Himself needed no repentance or cleansing from sin), becoming our substitute (2Cor 5:21). 4. His Baptism was an example to His followers.
3:16–17 All three persons of the Trinity are clearly seen here.
3:16 *Spirit of God.* The Holy Spirit came upon Jesus not to overcome sin (for He was sinless), but to equip Him (see note on Jdg 3:10) for His work as the divine-human Messiah.
3:17 An allusion to Ps 2:7 and Is 42:1.

Concordance

BAPTISM (BAPTIZE)
Mt   21:25 *b* of John, from where did it come?
Mk   1: 4 and proclaiming a *b* of repentance
       10:39 *b* with which I am baptized, you will
       11:30 Was the *b* of John from heaven or
Lk   3: 3 proclaiming a *b* of repentance
       12:50 I have a *b* to be baptized
       20: 4 was the *b* of John from heaven or
Ac   13:24 John had proclaimed a *b*
       18:25 he know only the *b*
       19: 3 They said, "Into John's *b*."

Ro   6: 3 who have been *b* into Christ Jesus
        6: 4 therefore with Him by *b*
Eph   4: 5 one Lord, one faith, one *b*,"
1Cor   1:16 did *b* also the household of.
1Cor   1:17 did not send me to *b*
Col   2:12 been buried with Him in *b*
2Pe   3:21 *B*, which corresponds to this,

A Model Prayer

Jesus gave the Lord's Prayer as a model for us to follow when we pray.

1. Use the concordance entry to find the location of the Lord's Prayer. *Hint: Jesus taught His disciples to pray the Lord's Prayer.*

Pray (Prayed, Prayer, Prayers, Praying, Prays)

1Sa 12:23 by ceasing to *p* for you.
2Ch 7:14 and *p* and seek My face
Ps 4: 1 be gracious to me and hear my *p*
   5: 2 and my God, for to you do I *p*.
     6:9 plea, and the Lord accepts my *p*
  32: 6 I who is godly offer *p* to you
 122: 6 *P* for the peace of Jerusalem!
 141: 2 Let my *p* be counted as incense,
Pr 15:29 He hears the *p* of the righteous.
Is 56: 7 poured out a whispered *p*
Mt 5:44 Love your enemies and *p* for,
  6: 5 "And when you *p*, you must
  6: 9 "*P* then like this: "Our Father:
 26:41 Watch and *p* that you may.
Mk11:25 And whenever you stand *p*,
 12:40 for a pretense make long *p*
Lk 5:16 to desolate places and *p*.
 11: 1 to Him, Lord, teach us to *p*
 18: 1 they ought always to *p*
 19:46 'My house shall be a house of *p*
Jn 17: 9 I am *p* for them. I am not
Ac 2:42 breaking of bread and the *p*
  6: 4 we will devote ourselves to *p*
 16:25 were *p* and singing hymns
Eph31:16 remembering you in my *p*
  6:18 *p* at all times in the Spirit,
Col 1: 9 we have not ceased to *p* for you
  4: 2 continue steadfastly in *p*
1Th 5:17 *p* without ceasing
2Th3: 1 Finally, brothers, *p* for us
Jas 5:13 Let him *p*. Is anyone
  5:16 and *p* for one another,
1Pe 3:7 so that your *p* may not be.
  4: 7 for the sake of your *p*.
Rv 5: 8 which are the *p* of the saints

2. Many Bibles include references in the margin between the two columns of verses printed on a page. These notes, identified by a small letter, list other verses in the Bible that include the word. Use the verses from the column notes to help you answer the following questions about this prayer. In the Bible from which this section is taken, the *S* (short for *See*) in the notes indicates that related information can be found in the verse that follows.

[9]Pray then like this:

> 'Our Father[a] in heaven,
> hallowed be your name.
> [10]Your kingdom[b] come,
> your will be done[c],
> on earth as it is in heaven.
> [11]Give us this day our daily bread,[d]
> [12]and forgive us our debts,
> as we also have forgiven our
> debtors[e].
> [13]And lead us not into temptation,
> but deliver us from evil[f].

column references:
6:9 [a]Jer 3:19; Mal 2:10; 1Pe 1:17
6:10 [b]S Mt 3:2 [c]S Mt 26:39
6:11 [d]Pr 30:8
6:12 [e]Mt 18:21-35
6:13 [f]Jas 1:13 S Mt 5:37

[f][13] Or *the evil one. Some late manuscripts add* for yours is the kingdom and the power and the glory forever. Amen.

6:10 *your kingdom come.* A reference to the future consummation of the kingdom.

6:11 *bread.* Represents the necessities, but not the luxuries of life.

6:12 *debts.* Moral debts, i.e., sins (see note on Lk 11:4).

  a. Why did God choose to have His followers call Him "Father" (see v. 9 above)?

  b. What does it mean to submit to the will of God?

  c. What does daily bread mean?

  d. How are being forgiven and forgiving related?

  e. What insights does the Book of James provide about temptation?

3. Now use the references or helps at the bottom of the example to give you more understanding. What new ideas do these sources give you?

4. Use all the resources above and write a paragraph about the Lord's Prayer. Be sure to include ideas of how you could model your prayers in this way. You might even write a prayer using the Lord's Prayer as your model.

Jesus and the Woman at the Well

Answer the following questions. Refer to the sheets titled "John 4:4–14" and "Samaria."

1. According to the Joshua reference accompanying verse 5, what claim to fame did Shechem have regarding the patriarch Jacob?

2. How else might the parenthetical phrase in verse 9 have been translated?

3. Why did the Jews and Samaritans generally not have a fond regard for each other? (See the dictionary entry for *Samaria*.)

4. Jesus referred to living water elsewhere in John (see margin references). According to the verse following the John references, what exactly is the living water Jesus offers?

5. In verse 10, Jesus tells the woman, "If you knew the gift of God, and who it is that is saying to you, 'Give Me a drink,' you would have asked Him, and He would have given you living water." Skim verses 15–26 of John 4. In which verse does Jesus tell the woman who He is?

6. What did the Samaritan woman mean when she referenced Jacob as "our father"? (See the dictionary entry regarding *Samaria*.)

7. See the map of Samaria. Where is the location of Jacob's well in relation to Jerusalem?

8. Jesus also referred to Samaritans in the story of the Good Samaritan. What was the intended destination of the traveler in the story of the Good Samaritan? (See the map; see also Luke 10:30.)

9. What center of worship for the Samaritans was located near Jacob's well? (See the map.)

10. What does Jesus' ministry to the Samaritan woman teach us about our attitude toward those we might be inclined to discriminate against?

John 4:4–14

⁴And He had to pass through Samaria.ᵉ ⁵So He came to a town of Samaria called Sychar, near the field that Jacob had given to his son Joseph.ᶠ ⁶Jacob's well was there; so Jesus, wearied as He was from His journey, was sitting beside the well. It was about the sixth hour.

⁷A woman from Samaria came to draw water. Jesus said to her, "Give Me a drink."ᵍ ⁸(For His disciples had gone away into the cityʰ to buy food.)

⁹The Samaritan woman said to Him, "How is it that You, a Jew, ask for a drink from me, a woman of Samariaⁱ?" (For Jews have no dealings with Samaritans.ᵇ)

¹⁰Jesus answered her, "If you knew the gift of God, and who it is that is saying to you, 'Give Me a drink,' you would have asked Him, and He would have given you living water."ʲ

¹¹The woman said to Him, "Sir, You have nothing to draw water with, and the well is deep. Where do You get that living water? ¹²Are You greater than our father Jacob? He gave us the wellᵏ and drank from it himself, as did his sons and his livestock."

¹³Jesus said to her, "Everyone who drinks of this water will be thirsty again, ¹⁴but whoever drinks of the water that I will give him will never be thirstyˡ again. The water that I will give him will become in him a spring of waterᵐ welling up to eternal life."ⁿ

ᵇOr *do not use dishes the Samaritans have used.*

4:4 ᵉS Mt 10:5
4:5 ᶠGe 33:19; Jos 24:32
4:7 ᵍGe 24:17; 1 Ki 17:10
4:8 ʰver 5, 39
4:9 ⁱS Mt 10:5
4:10 ʲIsa 44:3; 55:1; Jer 2:13; 17:13; Zec 14:8; Jn 7:37, 38; Rev 7:17; 21:6; 22:1, 17
4:12 ᵏver 6
4:14 ˡJn 6:35
ᵐIsa 12:3; 58:11; Jn 7:38
ⁿS Mt 25:46

4:4 *Samaria.* Here the whole region, not simply the city. Jews often avoided Samaria by crossing the Jordan and traveling on the east side (see notes on Mt 10:5; Lk 9:52).

4:5 *Sychar.* A small village near Shechem. Jacob bought some land near Shechem (Ge 33:18–19), and it was apparently this land that he gave to Joseph (Ge 48:21–22).

4:6 *Jacob's well.* This well is mentioned nowhere else in Scripture. *about the sixth hour.* About 12:00 noon.

4:7 *to draw water.* People normally drew water in the evening rather than in the heat of midday (see Ge 24:11 and note).

4:9 Jews would become ceremonially unclean if they used a drinking vessel handled by a Samaritan, since the Jews held that all Samaritans were "unclean."

4:10 *gift.* This Greek word is used only here in this Gospel and emphasizes God's grace through Christ. Jesus gave life and gave it freely. *living water.* In 7:38–39 the term is explained as meaning the Holy Spirit, but here it refers to eternal life (see v. 14).

4:11 *deep.* Ancient wells as deep as 100–135 feet have been found in this area.

4:12 *our father Jacob.* Regard for the past kept the woman from seeing the great opportunity of the present.

4:14 *welling up.* Jesus was speaking of vigorous, abundant life (cf. 10:10).

Samaria

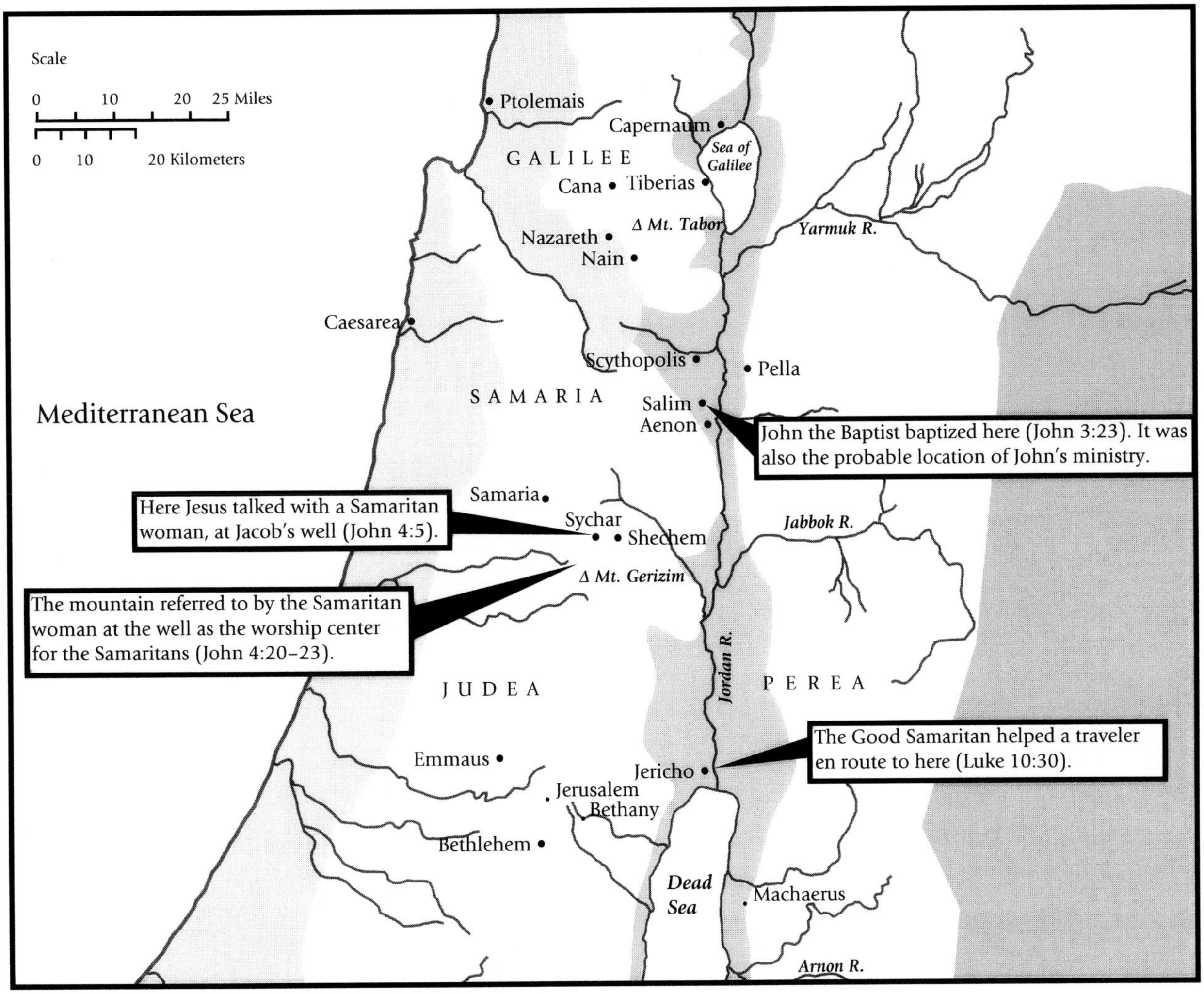

Scale
0 10 20 25 Miles
0 10 20 Kilometers
Ptolemais
Capernaum
Sea of Galilee
GALILEE
Cana
Tiberias
Mt. Tabor
Nazareth
Nain
Yarmuk R.
Caesarea
Scythopolis
Pella
SAMARIA
Mediterranean Sea
Salim
Aenon
John the Baptist baptized here (John 3:23). It was also the probable location of John's ministry.
Samaria
Here Jesus talked with a Samaritan woman, at Jacob's well (John 4:5).
Sychar
Shechem
Jabbok R.
Mt. Gerizim
The mountain referred to by the Samaritan woman at the well as the worship center for the Samaritans (John 4:20–23).
Jordan R.
PEREA
JUDEA
The Good Samaritan helped a traveler en route to here (Luke 10:30).
Emmaus
Jericho
Jerusalem
Bethany
Bethlehem
Dead Sea
Machaerus
Arnon R.

Dictionary Entry

Samaria: Region of Israel located between Galilee on the north and Judea on the south. After God's people were taken from this area into captivity, Assyrians brought in deportees from other countries to live alongside the Israelites who remained in this region. Eventually the people intermarried and became one group of people centered in Shechem. They practiced a religion blending pagan beliefs and the worship of the true God. When the people of God returned from captivity and began to rebuild the temple in Jerusalem, the Samaritans offered to help. God's people rejected their offer, and antagonism between the Jews and Samaritans resulted (see Ezra 4 and Nehemiah 2:10). Samaria is an agricultural region rich in wheat and barley and with grapes and olives produced on its gentle, sloping hills.

Answers

Page 4

(1) Bible; (2) Law; (3) Gospel; (4) messianic; (5) faith; (6) Holy Spirit; (7) wisdom; (8) prophets; (9) epistles

Page 5

(1) Moses; (2) Genesis, Exodus, Leviticus, Numbers, and Deuteronomy; (3) Paul; (4) Ruth; Esther; (5) Poetic

Page 6

(1) Acts; (2) Amos; (3) Daniel; (4) Deuteronomy; (5) Ecclesiastes; (6) Ezekiel; (7) Ezra; (8) Genesis; (9) Hosea; (10) John; (11) Lamentations; (12) Obadiah; (13) Nahum; (14) Nehemiah; (15) Numbers; (16) Philippians; (17) Philemon; (18) Proverbs; (19) Psalms; (20) Song of Solomon

Page 7

Narrative; Poetry; Prophecy; Apocalyptic

Page 8

Gospel—Daniel 12:1–3; Jeremiah 23:5–6; 1 John 1:7; John 3:16

Law—Isaiah 42:20; Amos 9:9–10; Ecclesiastes 7:20

Page 9

(1) Forth telling/Judgment; (2) Foretelling/Promise; (3) Foretelling/Promise; (4) Both/Promise; (5) Both/Promise; (6) Both/Promise; (7) Foretelling/Judgment; (8) Both/Promise

Page 10

(1) God's inspired Word; (2) Yes; the gifts of forgiveness, salvation, and power for godly living are gifts everyone needs; (3) God; (4) God's Word itself assures us.

Page 11

Malachi 3:1—W; Psalm 41:9—O; Isaiah 7:14—R; Isaiah 53:5—D; Psalm 22:1—A; Psalm 69:21—N; Micah 5:2—D; Zechariah 12:10—T; Zechariah 9:9–13—R; Isaiah 35:5–6—U; Jonah 1:17—T; Psalm 16:9–10—H. The letters combine to spell: WORD AND TRUTH.

Page 12

(1) In the temple; (2) Isaiah saw the Lord on His throne together with seraphs, or angels with six wings. (3) fearful, humbled; (4) This was a sign that Isaiah's sins were forgiven. (5) Serve as the Lord's messenger. (6) He was eager, ready to begin. (7) Through His prophet Isaiah, God called His people to repent of their sins. The people did not repent but rather continued to sin. (8) Even though God had scattered His people, He promised lovingly to bring them back.

Page 14

(1) Storm cloud with lightning and fire; (2) Responses will vary. (3) Very bright radiance; (4) Rebellious, obstinate, and stubborn; (5) Ezekiel ate the scroll containing God's words. The prophet is to preach judgment on Judah. God will give Ezekiel the right words to say. (6) Ezekiel will warn Judah of her sins and God's displeasure. (7) Everyone is held responsible for his or her own sins; however, each person is accountable for the death of those he or she did not warn about the consequences of their sin. (8) The Spirit of God; (9) Ezekiel shaved his head and destroyed all but a few of the shorn locks. God will utterly destroy Jerusalem but will preserve a faithful remnant. (10) A warning; (11) They will be destroyed. (12) They will know that the Lord is God. (13) Sword, famine, and plague; (14) The Lord is God. (15) God's glory departs from the temple. (16) God Himself is their sanctuary. (17) God will bring the exiles back to their homeland. (18) They will remove all false images and idols. (19) God will give them an undivided heart and a new spirit. (20) They will know and obey their God.

Page 15

Scene 1: (1) Without a Savior humanity is doomed. (2) Jesus is worthy to open the scroll (to assume His role as Savior). (3) Answers will vary.

Scene 2: (1a) Believers in heaven as a great number; (1b) They come from every people group. (2) White robes symbolize the cleanness of all who believe in Jesus. (3) In heaven, we will live in the presence of God in complete comfort, happiness, and peace—forever.

Scenes 3, 4, and 5: (1) Because God loves all people, He allows this world to continue so more people can come to faith. (2) God's people are shielded by His power from our enemies.

Scene 6: (1) We will enjoy a blissful relationship with our God and Savior. (2) Christ's promise can encourage and comfort us; He is coming soon!

Page 16

(1) c; (2) a; (3) b; (4) c; (5) a; Answers to second set of matchings will vary. All answers are acceptable.

Page 18

(1) "These are written so that you may believe that Jesus is the Christ, the Son of God, and that by believing you may have life in His name" (John 20:31). (2a) Showing Jesus as the descendant of both David and Abraham establishes Him as the promised Messiah. (2b) Mark was writing to the Romans who would not have been concerned about Jewish lineages. (2c) Luke's genealogy traces back to Adam. Luke emphasized the humanity of our Savior. (2d) John points to the eternal quality of God's Son—the Word made flesh.

Page 19

First section: Deeds—Jesus is baptized by John, tempted in the wilderness, calls His disciples, and ministers to crowds. Words—Jesus preaches His sermon on the mount.

Second section: Deeds—Jesus heals many, including a leper, a centurion's servant, two men with demons, and a paralytic; He calms a storm and calls Matthew to follow Him. He restores a girl to life and heals a woman, two blind men, and a man who was unable to speak. Words—Jesus sends out the Twelve after instructing them about the cost of discipleship.

Third section: Deeds—Jesus receives messengers sent from John the Baptist and heals a man with a withered hand. Words—Jesus speaks the parable of the sower, the parable of the weeds, and the parables of the mustard seed and the leaven, the hidden treasure, the pearl of great value, and that of the net.

Fourth section: Deeds—Jesus is rejected in Nazareth, feeds the crowd, walks on water, heals the sick, and heals the daughter of a Canaanite woman and many more. He also feeds another crowd, is transfigured, and heals a boy with a demon. Words—Jesus teaches about greatness, temptations, and about forgiveness. He speaks the parable of the lost sheep and the parable of the unforgiving servant.

Fifth section: Deeds—Jesus welcomes the children, interacts with the rich young man, heals two blind men, triumphantly enters Jerusalem, cleanses the temple. Words—Jesus teaches with the parables of the two sons, the tenants, and the wedding feast. Jesus speaks the seven woes to the Scribes and Pharisees and teaches about the end of all things. He speaks the parable of the ten virgins and of the talents.

Page 20

(1) g; (2) f; (3) e; (4) d; (5) b; (6) a; (7) c

Page 21

(1) Jesus prayed at His Baptism. (2) Crowds of people came to hear Jesus and to be healed. But Jesus often withdrew to lonely places and prayed. (3) Before calling His disciples, Jesus went out to a mountainside and spent the night praying to God. (4) Jesus gave thanks before performing the miracle of feeding the five thousand. (5) Once when Jesus was praying in private, He asked His disciples who the crowds said He was. (6) Jesus took Peter, James, and John onto a mountain to pray, and He was transfigured before them. (7) Full of joy through the Holy Spirit, Jesus praised God for hiding things from the wise and learned that He instead revealed to children. (8) One day after Jesus finished praying, His disciples asked Him to teach them to pray, and Jesus taught them the Lord's Prayer. (9) Jesus gave thanks before instituting the Sacrament of the Lord's Supper. (10) Jesus prayed for Simon (Peter) that his faith would not fail. (11) On the Mount of Olives, Jesus prayed according to His Father's will, asking that the cup of suffering might be removed from Him. (12) While on the cross, Jesus prayed for those who were crucifying Him. (13) After His resurrection, while seated with the disciples at Emmaus, Jesus took bread, gave thanks, and broke it.

Page 22

(1) f; (2) d; (3) e; (4) g; (5) a; (6) b; (7) c

Page 23

(1) Proverbs 6:23; (2) Proverb 1:8; (3) Titus 2:7; (4) 1 Timothy 5:17; (5) Acts 2:42; (6) 2 Timothy 4:3; (7) Acts 15:1

Page 24

(1) seek (2 Chronicles 15:2); (2) sinners (Galatians 2:17); (3) Jesus, perfecter, joy, shame throne; (Hebrews 12:2); (4) money, content, forsake; (Hebrews 13:5); (5) Son (John 8:36); (6) LORD, prisoners; (Psalm 146:7); (7) Christ, offering, sacrifice; (Ephesians 5:2)

Page 27

(1a) Exodus 6:6; (1b) 1—the LORD; 2—the people of Israel; (2a) Isaiah 54:5; Isaiah 54:8; (2b) Holy One of Israel; (3a) from the curse (of the law); (3b) by becoming a curse for us; (3c) adoption as sons; (4) God would have us return to Him; (5) Zechariah

Page 28

(1) Star by Ecclesiastes 12:3; (2) Cross by 1 John 5:3; (3) Answers will vary.

Page 31

(1) 13; (2) It is the only book in the Bible addressed to a woman. (3) John the apostle wrote the book sometime between AD 85 and 95. (4) Truth and love; (5) John warns against unintentionally supporting and assisting teachings that detract from or deny the truth.

Page 32

(1) John's greeting may be directed toward an actual Christian woman and her children. Or John may be speaking figuratively to a congregation and its members. (2) The word *truth* can be found five times in this epistle: twice in verse 1, once in verse 2, once in verse 3, once in verse 4. (3) The word *love* should be circled five times: once in verse 1, once in verse 3, once in verse 5, and twice in verse 6. (4) Followers of Jesus show their love for Him by walking in obedience to His commands (verse 6). (5a) Gnostics believed and taught that God's Son did not really become flesh but rather only temporarily came upon a man named Jesus between the time of His Baptism and His crucifixion. (5b) John describes the deceivers as those who do not acknowledge Jesus Christ as coming in the flesh. (6) Those who continue in Jesus' teaching are truly His disciples; they know the truth and the truth will make them free (John 8:32). (7) John associates joy with finding that some of the lady's children are walking in the truth (verse 4) and with the anticipation of being with a fellow believer in Jesus and talking with her face-to-face (v. 12).

Page 33

(1) Map; the Sea of Galilee and the Dead Sea; (2) Study Notes; Jesus was baptized to fulfill all righteousness, to be publicly proclaimed as the Messiah and to begin His ministry, to show Himself to be our substitute, and to provide His Baptism as an example for His followers. (3) Concordance: Mark 1:4—found in the concordance, John preached a Baptism of repentance for the forgiveness of sins. (4) Map; Bethany, Salim, and Scythopolis are near the Jordan River. (5) Study Notes for Matthew 3 and margin note for verse 16; not to overcome sin, because Jesus was—and is—sinless, but to equip Him for His work as the divine-human Messiah.

Page 34

(1) The Lord's Prayer is recorded in Matthew 6 and Luke 11. (2a) God treats us as His children, providing us with many good things. (2b) To submit to the will of God is to regard God's plans and desires above our own wants and wishes. (2c) When we pray for daily bread, we ask God to give us only what we need—neither poverty nor great wealth. (2d) God's people forgive generously because they have received generous forgiveness. (2e) God does not tempt anyone. Temptation has its origin in evil. (3) Answers will vary. (4) Answers will vary.

Page 35

(1) Jacob bought the tract of land at Shechem where his son Joseph was buried. The land became the inheritance of Joseph's descendants (Joshua 24:32). (2) Do not use dishes the Samaritans have used. (3) Samaritans were a mixture of peoples who practiced a blending of religious practices. Animosity between the two groups can be traced to the refusal of the people of God to allow the Samaritans to help them rebuild the temple. (4) The term "living water" refers to the Holy Spirit (John 7:39). (5) In John 4:26, Jesus clearly identifies Himself as the Messiah. (6) Like the Jews, the Samaritans were also descended from Jacob. (7) Samaria is located about 30 miles north of Jerusalem. (8) Jericho was the intended destination of the traveler. (9) Mt. Gerizim was the center of Samaritan worship. (10) God would have us value all people as those for whom Christ has died.